Law of Attraction for Abundance

How to Change Your Relationship with Money to Manifest the Wealth You Truly Desire

By Elena G.Rivers

Copyright Elena G.Rivers © 2017

www.LOAforSuccess.com

Contents

Introduction

I remember watching a cartoon as a child where a man was making his way across the desert. He struggled as he walked under the merciless sun. All that he could think about was having water to drink. He felt like each step that he took would be his last when suddenly he saw an oasis in the distance. Excited, he ran toward the oasis. As he got closer to the oasis, it began to fade until it disappeared. Instead of life-giving water, there was just more desert sand.

Midas was well-known for his greediness. He wanted to be the wealthiest man in the world. In Greek mythology, there is the story of Midas, the king of Phrygia.

One day, Midas performed an act that pleased the god Dionysus. In return for his thoughtful gesture, Dionysus offered to grant Midas the wish of his choice. Midas told Dionysus that he wanted to be able to turn anything he touched into gold. Dionysus warned Midas of the dangers of such a wish; however, Midas persisted with his request. Unable to refuse Midas, Dionysus hesitantly granted Midas his wish.

Midas was thrilled with his new powers. Everything that he touched turned into gold. He had the "Midas touch." He now could become the wealthiest man in the world. However, the thrill of his new gift was short-lived. Midas realized that he was unable to eat or drink, for they also turned to gold.

Both the man traveling through the desert and the story of King Midas are metaphors for two different mindsets toward money. Like the man traveling across the desert, many of us struggle financially and are searching for the opportunity to quench our thirst for financial stability or wealth. Unfortunately, it never appears. There are others who are like King Midas who pursue money with a laser-like focus and end up being cursed.

Regardless of our intentions for wanting more money, most of us pursue the traditional approach, which is to expend a great deal of energy at the expense of others or ourselves.

This book was written to provide a radically different perspective on success. And not just financial success, but success in all areas of our lives. The perspective this book takes is through the Law of Attraction. There are plenty of books on the market about the Law of Attraction. However, this book is different.

Because it's written from a higher perspective, this book provides insights that most other books on the Law of Attraction fail to address.

They fail to address these insights because they are written from a dualistic perspective. This book begins with a discussion on higher levels of consciousness and works downward to the nuts and bolts of attracting anything that you could desire, especially money.

By adopting the principles in this book and consistently applying them, you will be able to transform your life. All that's required for this transformation is to have an open mind, an open heart, and the determination to challenge some of your most deep-seated beliefs.

A Special Free Offer from Elena to Help You Manifest Faster

The best way to get in touch with me is by joining my free email newsletter.

You can easily do it in a few seconds by visiting our private website at:

www.LOAforSuccess.com/newsletter

The best part?

When you sign up, you will instantly receive a free copy of an exclusive **LOA Workbook** that will help you raise your vibration in 5 days or less:

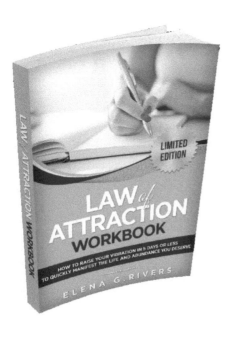

Chapter 1: The Secret Behind the Secret

The 2006 bestseller, *The Secret,* introduced a mass audience to the Law of Attraction. *The Secret* was well-received because the timing was right. The timing was right because universal consciousness is continually evolving, and it reached a point where *The Secret* resonated with us.

However, *The Secret,* and many other books on the Law of Attraction, only examined the Law of Attraction from a surface level. Because of this, a lot of crucial information was not communicated; information that you need to know to more effectively use the Law of Attraction.

That this information was not contained in *The Secret* was not due to ignorance on the part of the author. Rather, it was written to conform to our dualistic understanding of the world. The purpose of this book is to pick up where *The Secret* left off and provide you with that vital information so that you can use the Law of Attraction to more effectively attract wealth into your life.

To do so, we will first explore the non-dualistic view of life so that we can understand the Law of Attraction, and ourselves, from a broader context. Using this understanding, we will explore practical steps you can take to develop a mindset that is more open to attracting and receiving money with less frustration and mental energy. We will start by exploring our relationship with consciousness itself.

Chapter 2: From Nothing to Something

What is the source of existence? Where did we come from? What is the true nature of reality? These are the big questions that philosophers, scholars, poets, and scientists have pondered through the ages.

Though it may seem that the answers to these questions are out of reach, I believe that we are much closer than we think.

In many religious faiths, the answer to these questions would be God. In Buddhism, which does not believe in an external deity, it would be Ku. Ku is the essential aspect of existence. It is formless, timeless, and non-changing. In other words, it cannot be perceived by our senses and is beyond our ability to comprehend.

From it arises everything that we experience, including us. In quantum physics, there is the quantum field, which has the qualities of Ku and is made of energy. From religion to quantum physics, it appears that everything that is known arises from the formless. In this book, I will refer to this source of everything as consciousness. Consciousness is the awareness that creates all of existence.

Everything that we experience arises from consciousness. The water cycle is a helpful metaphor for understanding how consciousness manifests into form. Water in its gaseous state cannot be perceived by us. The air contains water in its gaseous state. When the moisture in the air cools, it condenses and forms clouds. When the moisture in the clouds becomes saturated, it becomes rain. When rain is exposed to cool enough temperatures, it becomes ice. In this manner, water in its formless state manifests into the form that we know as rain or ice. Regardless of its form, water's essential nature remains the same, which is two hydrogen atoms and one oxygen atom.

Consciousness is a form of intelligence and information and has the infinite potential to express itself, which it does to expand. To expand, consciousness needs to experience itself. What we refer to as manifestation is consciousness expanding, and the expansion process begins with desire. Desire is the genesis of physical manifestation. Consciousness manifests desire from the information that it receives from our sense of experience. Desire manifests as thought, which we experience as the mind. Thought manifests as emotion, which motivates us. Emotion manifests as action, and action creates the effects that we experience. The effects that we experience create new desires in us, which completes the manifestation cycle and the expansion of consciousness.

Like gas, consciousness is formless, or non-phenomenal, and expresses itself as the phenomenal. The term "phenomenal" refers to that which we can perceive through our mind and senses, while non-phenomenal refers to that which we cannot perceive. Desires, thoughts, emotions, and action are phenomenal.

Because we identify with these phenomena, we experience ourselves as the mind and body. Because we experience ourselves as a mind and body, we experience ourselves as being separate from our surroundings. Because we experience ourselves as being separate from our surroundings, we experience contrast. Because we experience contrast, we can have experiences. Here is an example of what I mean:

I am a physical expression of consciousness, which is my essential nature. Because I experience myself as being a separate being, I experience the world as "me and other." I am "me," and everything else that I experience is "other." I am not my home, my family, my dog, or my car; all of these things are perceived to be something outside of myself. Because I see myself as being separate from these things, I experience contrast. I can see how my home is different from me. I can see how my family is different from me, and so on. That contrast creates experience.

My experience appears to me in the form of thought. It is my thoughts that inform consciousness of my experience.

My thoughts, which result from experience, inform consciousness, which allows it to experience itself. By experiencing itself, it creates new potentials that are consistent with the information that it receives. Here is another example:

I, who sees myself as a separate being, sees my car parked next to a fancy sports car. Seeing my old Toyota next to this shiny new sports car creates contrast. I can see the major differences between the two vehicles. This contrast leads to an experience, which may appear as thoughts such as:

- I need to wash my car.
- *I am going to save my money to buy a car like that.*
- I will never be able to afford a car like that.

These thoughts inform consciousness which then manifests as phenomena that are consistent with my thoughts. If my previous thought was, "I need to wash my car," then all the conditions that are needed for me to wash my car will appear.

If my thoughts are, "I am going to save my money to buy a car like that," consciousness will manifest conditions that make this possible. It is this attracting of conditions that match our thoughts that is known as the Law of Attraction. As our essential selves, the Law of Attraction does not exist because the nature of consciousness is "oneness."

It is only in our phenomenal form, which is characterized by a sense of separateness that the Law of Attraction exists.

The level of our ability to use the Law of Attraction is dependent on how effectively we can align our phenomenal self with our essential self.

Chapter 3: The Illusion of Separation

As you read this book, you most likely experience yourself as being separate from the book. You also probably experience yourself as separate from that which you are sitting on. You also most likely experience yourself as different from your environment.

Except for light and sound, everything that you experience, including yourself, is made of molecules. Molecules are made of atoms. In fact, the carbon atom is the basic atom of all living and non-living beings.

Once thought to be the fundamental unit of matter, we now know that the atom is not solid. Rather, the atom is made of subatomic particles that are separated by vast distances of space. Additionally, the subatomic particles are not solid. Atoms are fluctuations of energy.

What this means is that, at the most fundamental level, there is no difference between you, this book, your electronic device, and your environment. Further, you and this book are no more solid than the air around you. At the atomic level, you and the money that you desire are one in the same. At the most fundamental level, everything is energy.

The cause of our experience of separation is our identification with the mind and body's functions. We experience ourselves having thoughts, perceptions, emotions, and feelings. We also experience ourselves as having a body that appears to be solid.

Because of how we experience the mind and body, we believe that we *are* the mind and body. Everything else that we experience is perceived to be something separate from ourselves, including the money that we desire.

Here are some exercises to challenge your perceptions of being separate from the world:

Exercise 1
Note: It is recommended that you first review this and other meditations in this book before performing them as they contain a lot of information. Another alternative is to read them out loud while recording them and then play them back when you are ready to meditate.

In this meditation, you will have the opportunity to challenge the nature of experience itself. When conducting this exercise, do not involve your knowledge or thinking. Rely solely on your immediate and direct experience.

1. Sit down and view your surroundings, taking your time to take everything in.

2. When you are ready, close your eyes and allow yourself to relax.

3. Imagine that you are an alien from a distant planet who has arrived on Earth to study it. You have no information about this planet, nor do you have any experience to draw from. Because of this, you are unable to define, identify, analyze, or judge anything that you experience. In other words, you are a blank slate.

4. Now, open your eyes and look at your surroundings again. Take your time.

5. How did your experience observing compare with your first observation?

If you did not notice any difference between the two observations, practice this exercise until you do. When we impose our thoughts on that which we are experiencing, what we are experiencing becomes a reflection of our thoughts.

Thought reconfigures everything that we experience. It is for this reason that Buddhism teaches us that our environment is a mirror of our inner world. Being able to observe without utilizing conceptual thinking is being mindful and present.

Exercise 2

Note: When conducting this exercise, do not involve your knowledge or thinking. Rely solely on your immediate and direct experience.

1. Sit down and make yourself comfortable. Allow yourself to relax. If you would like, you may close your eyes for now.

2. Allow yourself to relax as you focus on your breathing. Place your attention on your breath as it enters your body, travels through your body, and then leaves it as you exhale.

3. Breathe normally without exerting any effort. Relax.

4. When you are ready, open your eyes.

5. Now, look at an object in your surroundings.

6. As you look at the object, ask yourself, "Does seeing occur outside of me or from within me?" I hope you agree that seeing occurs from within you.

7. Does seeing require any thought or effort?

For most of us, the answer to both of these questions would be "no." Even a blind person can "see" mental images.

8. Now, look at the object again. Ask yourself the following question: Does seeing stop at the point where the object begins, or does the object being seen and the act of seeing flow into each other?

    I hope you will agree that seeing and the object being seen flow into each other.

9. How do you know that seeing is taking place? You know that seeing is taking place because you are aware of it.

10. Now, ask yourself whether you can separate the awareness of seeing from the act of seeing. I hope you agree that the awareness of seeing and the act of seeing are inseparable.

By practicing this exercise, I hope that you realize that seeing an object, the act of seeing, and the awareness that seeing is taking place are inseparable. They are one in the same.

That the act of seeing seems to originate from within us, and the object being seen appears to be outside of us, is an illusion created by the mind. From higher levels of perspective, there is no "inside" or "outside." You and what you experience are inseparable from each other.

You can repeat this exercise by replacing "seeing" with "hearing" or "touching. With enough practice, you will inevitably realize that who you are cannot be separate from the world around you.

Thought leads us to believe that we are separate from life. When we base our understanding on our direct experience, we find that we can never be separate from life, including the money that we desire to attract.

Exercise 3

The following exercise is similar to the preceding one, but it involves the senses of touch and hearing. As with the previous exercise, it is intended to challenge how you perceive the world around you. When conducting this exercise, do not involve your knowledge or thinking. Rely solely on your immediate and direct experience.

1. Sit down and close your eyes.

2. Now, touch your leg. As you touch your leg, ask yourself, "Am I experiencing my leg, or am I experiencing the sensation of touching my leg?"
3. I hope that you agree that you are experiencing the sensation of touching your leg.
4. Now ask yourself, is sensation experienced outside of me or within me?
5. I hope you agree that sensation is experienced within you, just as in seeing.
6. How do you know sensation is being experienced? You know of sensation because there is an awareness of it.
7. Now, listen to a sound in your environment. When you hear a specific sound, do not attach a label to it. In other words, if you hear a bird singing, do not think, "A bird is singing." Instead, just listen to the sound that it makes without thinking about it.
8. As you listen to the sound, touch your leg again. As with listening, do not attach any labels or think about it. You only want to experience the sensation. Are the sound that you hear and the sensation that you feel separate from each other?

Practice this exercise (with your eyes closed) until you reach the realization that both sensation and sound are aspects of experience that appears in your awareness. Sensation and sound appear in awareness and are indivisible from each other.

When we do not conceptualize our experience, meaning that we do not label or think about it, we realize that all we can ever know is experience and our awareness of it. Further, awareness is indivisible from experience itself. Your direct experience of this will give you a major advantage in manifesting. The reason why is this: Everything that you could want already exists in your life.

All challenges in manifesting through the Law of Attraction are the result of us putting our attention on our sense of separateness. If there is anything that you desire that is not currently evident in your life, it is because you have not made yourself open enough to receive it. The reason why we are not open to receiving is that we see ourselves as being separate from it.

At the level of our ordinary awareness, we believe that we can use the Law of Attraction to attract money into our lives, or that we have to do it the old fashion way, which is to work at it. From the perspective of higher levels of awareness, having the desire for money is enough to manifest it in our lives if we do not prevent ourselves from receiving it. To become effective manifesters, we need to adopt a mindset that is consistent with consciousness.

The degree that we can manifest is dependent on our alignment with consciousness, which we will be exploring in the upcoming chapters. But before we do, let us explore the most essential tool for understanding the manifestation process. That tool is meditation.

Chapter 4: Meditation

Meditation is an essential tool for increasing awareness of the nature of the mind and overcoming the illusions of reality that it creates. Most of us have lost our inward focus and concentrate on the outer realm that surrounds us, which is what we refer to as the world. Meditation makes it possible for us to see beyond this illusion of separation and realize that the outer realm is reflecting our inner realm.

We will use meditation techniques throughout this book to expand our awareness of the nature of the mind. For now, here is a simple meditation to practice that will build the foundation for the upcoming meditative exercises.

Basic Meditation

1. Find a quiet place to sit that is comfortable. You may sit either on the floor or in a chair.
2. Close your eyes and allow yourself to relax by placing your attention on the flow of your breath. Keep your awareness on your breath as you inhale by focusing on the sensations. Do the same thing during exhalation by placing your attention on the sensations that are experienced as your breath travels out of your body. Breathe naturally; it is vital that you make no effort at

any time during this meditation. An alternative to following your breath is to focus on the rising and falling of your abdomen.

3. Keep your focus on your breathing. If at any time you catch your mind wandering, just return your attention to the sensations of your breath. Do this as often as necessary without any form of judgment of yourself.

By continuing to practice this meditation, you will increase your awareness to the coming and fading of thought. By focusing on your breathing, you deprive your thoughts of the attention that you have been giving them; thus, slowing down your mental activity.

Chapter 5: The Vibrational Universe

You and I are multidimensional beings in that we are simultaneously non-phenomenal and phenomenal. Our essential self is consciousness while our experience of being a person is the manifestation of consciousness.

Your manifested self is the aspect of you that can have an experience. Your essential self, which is consciousness, creates new manifestations based on the information that it gains from your experiences. The information that is gained from experience takes on the form of thought.

The quality of our thoughts determines the quality of manifestations that are expressed by our essential self. More specifically, the quality of the thoughts that we focus on determines the quality of the manifestations that are expressed by consciousness.

In the following chapters, we will discuss the role of thoughts in the manifestation process as well as the roles of emotions and feelings. However, before we discuss these mental functions, we need to understand the vibrational nature of reality.

While consciousness is the essence of existence, everything that is expressed by consciousness is a vibrational expression of it. To better understand this, we can go back to the water cycle as a metaphor. Water can take on the form of a gas, liquid, or solid. What determines the form that water takes is the behavior of its molecules.

In the gaseous state, water molecules are further apart than in any other state. The reason why water is invisible as a gas is because of the great distances between its molecules. Not only are the molecules far apart from each other, but they are also very active and vibrate at a high frequency.

When water becomes a liquid, the molecules are closer together but still have a lot of distance between them. It is for this reason that water, as a liquid, can flow and take on the shape of the container that it is in. As a liquid, the molecules are active and vibrate at a high frequency, though its activity and vibrational frequency are lower than that of gas.

When water becomes solid, the molecules are close together. It is the close proximity of the molecules that give ice its solid form. Because of their proximity, the molecules are far less active than liquid water and have a low vibrational rate.

Just as with water, the different manifestations of consciousness also have a vibrational quality to them. Thoughts, feelings, emotions, and the physical body are different vibrational qualities of the consciousness.

Only consciousness is conscious. The mind, thoughts, feelings, emotions, and physical body are not conscious. Our phenomenal selves are experienced by us within the field of consciousness, so we believe that our phenomenal self is conscious. Thoughts, emotions, and feelings are the vibrational qualities of conscious energy that we experience in our phenomenal form. In this manner, the only difference between a thought and a pile of money is the vibrational level.

Thoughts

Imagine that you go to the Grand Canyon and see the mighty Colorado River. The river is vast with torrential waters that travel through the canyon at high speeds. Now imagine that you take an eye dropper and place it in the river to collect a sample of its water. We would never confuse the water sample with the river. However, most of us confuse thought with reality.

The Colorado River is a metaphor for consciousness. Consciousness is infinite, without boundaries or limits. All information that has ever existed, or will exist, is found within consciousness. In our manifested form, we can tap into consciousness for information. Just as with dipping an eyedropper into the Colorado River, the information that we receive from consciousness is just a minute sample of reality.

Not only is it a tiny sample, but it is also subjectively influenced by our past conditioning. For example, the thoughts that we have for a piece of art is distorted by our past experiences. One person may see a piece of artwork as being brilliant while another may find it to be nonsense.

Thoughts lack any power that is inherently their own. Rather, they become energized by us giving attention to them. When we give thoughts our attention, they become our reality. The popular adage that we create our reality cannot be understated.

Our reality consists of the thoughts that we identify with.

When we have a sense of certainty about our thoughts, we refer to them as beliefs. Our beliefs define our experience of reality. Because we have such a sense of certainty about our beliefs, we are unable to perceive anything that lies outside of them. If I believe that I will never experience a million dollars, I will never notice the opportunities to make a million dollars.

One aspect of aligning our manifested self with our essential self is transforming our limiting beliefs.

Exercises for Beliefs

Identifying limiting beliefs

The following are exercises that can be used to identify or change your limiting beliefs:

Exercise 4

To show you how this exercise works, I will provide you with an example.

1. Think of an ongoing challenge that you are experiencing in your life. For my example, I will use: "I can never get ahead financially."

2. My next step is to start a line of inquiry using the phrase, "What would be so bad if..." So my first question would be, "What would be so bad about not getting ahead financially?"

3. My answer to that question would be, "I will continue to struggle."

4. I would then use my response and rephrase the question: "What would be so bad if I continue to struggle financially?"

5. My response to that would be, "I will never feel financially secure."

6. I would continue to repeat this question by asking: "What would be so bad if I do not feel finically secure?"

7. My answer to that would be, "I would feel inadequate or like a failure."

8. Keep going through this line of questioning until you are unable to go any further. When you have reached this point, you will have identified your subconscious belief. At the conscious level, my challenge was that I cannot get ahead financially. At a deeper level, my challenge is that I feel inadequate and that I am a failure. For me to attract wealth, I need to transform my belief that I am inadequate and a failure. My difficulty in getting ahead financially is just a symptom of this.

Exercise 5:

This next exercise can be used to find the subconscious beliefs about the things that we want. For this exercise, I will use the example: "I want to be rich."

1. What would getting rich give me?

2. It would give me a sense of financial security.

3. What would having a sense of financial security give me?

4. It would make me feel more relaxed.

5. What would feeling more relaxed give me?

6. It would give me a sense of peace.

7. My subconscious belief is that I want a sense of peace, but my conscious belief is that I want to be rich.

Changing a Belief

Exercise 6:

When you have identified a belief that is limiting you, you can use the following procedure to weaken your old belief and replace it with a more empowering one:

1. Get two sheets of paper. Select paper sizes 8" x 11" or larger.
2. Take the first sheet of paper and fold it in half lengthwise.
3. At the top, write down your belief.
4. Make a list on the left-hand side of all the ways this belief has cost you in your life. When doing this part of the exercise, think of how this belief has affected you in all of your life areas. Ask yourself how living by this belief has affected the way that you see yourself, how it has affected your emotional health, relationships, physical health, work, finances, and so on.
5. When writing, keep in mind:
   a. Write down the first thing that comes to your mind, even if it seems irrelevant.

b. Write as fast as you can and feel the emotions that arise. This is a heartfelt exercise, not a thinking one.

c. Keep writing until you run out of things to write.

6. Next to each item that you write down, assign an arbitrary point value as to how much impact this item has had on you. When selecting a point value, choose the first number that comes to mind.

7. When you have completed assigning the point values, find the total of all the point values and place it at the bottom of the page.

8. For the right side of the page, repeat Steps 4-7, except this time, you will write down all of the ways that this belief has benefited you.

When you have completed Step 8, think of a new alternative belief that empowers you. For example, if the original belief was, "I will never enjoy financial success," my new belief may be, "Financial success is just an expression of who I am that I have not yet tapped into."

On the second paper, repeat steps 1-8 using your new belief with the following exceptions: Reverse Steps 4 and 8 by writing down all the ways that you believe that you would benefit from this new belief for Step 4. When doing Step 8, write down all the ways you think that it will cost you.

When you have completed the two sheets, do the following:

1. Immediately review your lists, allowing yourself to experience any emotions that arise.
2. Review your lists every day, once in the morning and once before you go to bed until you become fully associated with the emotions that you experience.

When you become associated with the costs of holding on to your old belief with the benefits of adopting your new belief, your mind will become re-programmed with your new belief.

Emotions

I previously offered the metaphor of the water cycle with its different phases of water's manifestation as a gas, liquid, or solid.

If thought is like water's gas phase, emotions are like the liquid form. What we call "emotions" are the next level of manifestation from thought. Emotions are the tangible expression of our thoughts. They are the universe's way of making our thoughts more evident to us.

Though we have many thoughts, our thoughts are just indicators of whether or not we have a pleasurable or painful experience. The thought, "I will never be rich," can be a painful thought, which alerts my nervous system to this understanding. Conversely, the thought, "I can attract wealth if I have the proper mindset," is pleasurable and will register in my nervous system in that way.

The crucial thing to understand is that neither thought is inherently true. They are just interpretations that our minds make out of the information that it receives from consciousness.

Because we are not always able to identify the thoughts that we are experiencing, especially our subconscious thoughts, our emotions provide a palpable message to the quality of our thoughts. If I am experiencing happiness, it is because I am having thoughts of the same quality. If I am experiencing anger, it is because I am having thoughts of that nature.

We experience a range of emotions with each having its own vibrational frequency.

At the low end of the spectrum are feelings such as shame, humiliation, or guilt. Further up the spectrum are things like disappointment, anxiousness, or fear. While low in their vibrational frequency, they are higher than the first category of emotions because they are more likely to lead us to take action.

Next up the spectrum are emotions like anger, determination, and pride. These emotions have a vibrational frequency that is higher than the last category, and they are more likely to cause us to take action to change our situation.

Going further up the spectrum are the emotions of happiness, allowing, and acceptance. These have a higher frequency than the ones below them because they are further away from the vibration of fear.

The feelings of gratitude and appreciation are even higher than the previous category because they cause us to have a more outward focus than the previous categories.

The last categories centered on how we feel about our situation; they inform us as to whether our situation is pleasurable or if we need to avoid it.

Gratitude and appreciation cause us to focus less on our situation and more on the object of our gratitude and appreciation. I can have gratitude because I see that I live a higher standard of living than most people in other parts of the world. Appreciation has a higher vibration than gratitude because gratitude implies that we are grateful for something that we received. Appreciation can be experienced without having received something in return. In other words, it can be unconditional. I can have an appreciation for a beautiful flower or the work of artists.

Exercises for the Mindfulness of Emotions

The following meditative exercises will allow you to develop a greater awareness of your emotions and how to transform them.

Exercise 7

The purpose of this meditation is to develop a greater awareness of your emotions.

1. Find a quiet place where you will not be disturbed and make yourself comfortable.

2. When relaxed, close your eyes and place your attention on your breath. For approximately one minute, use your attention to follow the path of your breath as it enters your body during inhalation and leaves it during exhalation. Do not put any effort into this. Simply observe your breath flowing through you. If you wish to extend this step for more than one minute, feel free to do so.

3. Adopt the attitude that you will allow anything that you experience to exist without any involvement by you. Do not resist or try to change anything. Let everything that appears do so without judging it.

4. If you experience an unpleasant thought or emotion, allow yourself to observe it like a birdwatcher observes a rare bird from a distance. Do not try to interfere in any way with the unpleasant emotion. Do not give any thought or concern to it. Simply observe it calmly without getting involved.

5. As you observe the thought or emotion, what happens to it? Does it get weaker and fainter? The change in potency happens because you are no longer engaging with these mental functions. Like thoughts, emotions depended on you for their power.

Exercise 8

The purpose of this meditation is to become more deeply aware of the nature of your emotions:

1. Sit down and make yourself comfortable.

2. Close your eyes and allow yourself to relax.

3. Place your attention on your breath as it enters and exits your body, focusing on the sensations you experience as you inhale and exhale.

4. Identify any negative emotions that you might be experiencing. If you are not experiencing a negative emotion, think of a problem or negative experience. When you experience a negative emotion, offer it total

acceptance. Do not try to avoid it, deny it, or change it. Allow the emotion to fully express itself.

5. Place your full awareness on the emotion. Allow yourself to observe it with your attention, but do not engage it. Allow yourself to experience the sensations that accompany the emotion. Pretend that you are diving into the emotion and allow yourself to become fully immersed in it. Remember, your emotions have no power as long as you do not try to resist them to or try to interpret them. As long as your involvement with them is restricted to observing and experiencing them, you will be in charge.

6. What happens to the potency of your emotions when you just observe them and allow them to express themselves?

Exercise 9

1. Sit in a comfortable position and close your eyes.

2. Allow yourself to follow your breath during inhalation and exhalation. Place your attention on your breath. Feel it as it courses through your body.

3. Take on an attitude of complete allowing. Whatever arises in this meditation, you will have complete acceptance of it.

4. Observe the perceptions, thoughts, sensations, feelings, and emotions that arise within you. Allow them to come and go on their own. All you need to do is be the observer of them.

5. Now, pay attention to any emotion that arises. Become an observer of it. What happens when your focus is placed on your emotion?

6. Do not place any meaning on the emotion you experience. Do not think of it as being positive or negative. Words such as "positive," "negative," "pleasant," or "unpleasant" are products of the mind

7. There is no intrinsic meaning to anything in life. All meaning is derived from our minds. Emotions and feelings have no power of their own. They derive their power from the attention we give them.

8. When observing emotions, do so with complete allowing. Do not try to change anything about it.

9. As you observe your emotions, do you notice a change in how you experience them? Do they change in intensity? Do they become stronger or milder? Can you locate where the emotions came from? Can you observe where they go?

10. As you observe emotions, ask yourself, "Am I my emotions, or am I the one that is aware of them?" If a feeling or emotion is experienced as being unpleasant, does awareness feel unpleasant? If an emotion is

experienced as being pleasant, does awareness feel pleasant?

11. Awareness does not experience anything; it can only know of experience. Awareness is like a beam of light shining on a snow-covered field. The light does not feel the cold of the snow, it only illuminates it. As you observe emotions, become the beam of light.

12. This is the end of this meditation. Feel free to remain in meditation for as long as you wish.

Exercise 10

The purpose of this exercise is to transform your emotions once you have become comfortable with the previous exercises. It will involve you playing a more active role than in the previous exercises, and it is a powerful tool if you have a strong negative emotion that has been lingering in you. Do the following:

1. Sit down and make yourself comfortable.

2. Place your attention on your breath as it enters and exits your body, focusing on the sensations you experience as you inhale and exhale.

3. If you are not already experiencing a negative emotion, relive a memory that will activate one. Think of a

negative experience from the past or one that you are currently experiencing.

4. When the negative emotion appears, identify what the emotion feels like. Remember, you want to describe what the emotion feels like, not what you think about it. To avoid falling into this trap, phrase your response, "It feels like_____."

Here are some examples:
- "It feels like there is a weight on me."
- "I feel like I want to hide."
- "It leaves me feeling defeated."
- "It feels like I am being crushed."

After you identify what the emotion feels like, use the following process to transform your emotion using your response from Step 4. Here is an example:

1. If the emotion that I am feeling is anger, my response to what anger feels like would be, "It feels like my I am going to explode."
2. I would then repeat the process by asking, "What does exploding feel like?
3. My response to that would be, "It feels like tension is filling my body."

4. I would follow up with, "What does tension feel like?"
5. With every response that I give, I would repeat the same line of questioning until the emotion transforms into a positive emotion.

The key to this exercise is to become fully associated with the emotions that you experience. Also, when trying to identify the feeling of the emotion, go by the first answer that comes to you.

Do not worry about getting it wrong; you can't. As long as you describe the feeling of the emotion without getting intellectual about it, you will be on the right track.

Every time you describe an emotion, you allow it to transform itself. By continuously describing it every time that it transforms, the emotion will eventually transform into a positive emotion. Using this process allows the emotion to go full circle and heal itself.

When you learn to transform your emotions, you will automatically transform your thoughts. By transforming your thoughts in a way that feels empowering to you, you will improve your alignment with consciousness, which is your essential self.

Feelings and Sensations

Our thoughts and emotions are forms of conscious energy that become altered by our past conditioning. For example, I may feel angry, but I would never harm another person or animal. However, some people would. Why do I act differently under anger than some other people? It is because of my past conditioning, which is based on how I was raised, the norms of the society that I grew up in, and my experiences. All of these things created my conditioning.

There is a conscious energy that is pure and unaltered by my personal experience, and that conscious energy is my feelings. Our feelings are our direct connection to consciousness. For this reason, our feelings are like our GPS for determining our alignment with our essential selves.

Anytime we experience feelings of well-being, we are in alignment with our essential selves. Anytime that we are not experiencing the feelings of well-being, it means that we are out of alignment. Many of us have lost touch with the feelings of the body because we are preoccupied with our thoughts, or we are trying to avoid our feelings because we find them threatening to our emotional being. The following exercises will help you increase your awareness to the feelings and sensations that you experience in your body.

Exercise 11

1. Close your eyes and allow yourself to follow your breath during inhalation and exhalation. Place your attention on your breath. Feel it as it courses through your body.

2. Now, place your attention on the sensations of your body. Place your attention on any sensation that appears in your awareness.

3. Do you feel a tingling in your hands or feet? Do you feel tensions in your back, shoulders, or face? Do you feel the weight of your body or the pressure on your buttocks from the chair or ground that you are sitting on?

4. Allow yourself to experience the sensations of the body without any judgment, even ones that may feel unpleasant. There are no good or bad sensations. Good and bad, pleasant and unpleasant, these are value judgments that exist solely in mind. The same thing is true with perceptions, sounds, and thoughts. They just exist.

5. Are the sensations that you experience stable? Are they always the same, or do they change? Are they always there, or do they come and go?

6. Just stay in the awareness of your body's sensations. Allow yourself to experience them for as long as you desire.

7. This is the end of this meditation. Please feel free to allow yourself to continue to meditate on the body for as long as you wish.

For many of us, there is a lack of awareness of our inner world. This is because we spent most of our waking hours focusing on the world outside of ourselves. For the same reasons, we often lack an awareness of our bodies. We may be unaware of subtle sensations and feelings. The body is the interface that allows consciousness to experience the physical world. In fact, the physical body plays a vital role in allowing us to develop greater levels of consciousness.

Exercise 12

Most instructions for meditation advise you to sit in a comfortable position while sitting in an upright position. One of keys to meditation is learning to be allowing of all experiences and to not control anything, including your body. In this meditation, you will listen to the body and allow it to move or position itself in complete freedom.

1. Sit down and make yourself comfortable. Allow yourself to relax.
   Close your eyes and focus on your breath. Allow yourself to become relaxed.

2. Forget about what you learned from your mother about sitting straight. If your body feels like slumping over, let it. Allow your body to do whatever it wants.

3. Place your awareness on your body and its sensations. Let your awareness be soft and do not get caught up in your thinking.

4. Observe the sensations of the body and any messages that you are getting.

5. Honor the messages from the body by allowing it to express itself freely.

6. This is the end of this meditation. Feel free to allow yourself to listen to your body for as long as you desire.

Exercise 13

In this meditation, you will experience the power of awareness on the body.

1. Sit down and make yourself comfortable, if you like, you can close your eyes.

2. Place your attention on your breath as it travels in and out of your body. Allow your awareness to wash over your body and experience the sensations.

3. Now, scan your body with your awareness for a relaxed, calm, or pleasant sensation. When you find such a sensation, allow yourself to focus on it.

4. As you observe this sensation, I want you to ask yourself the following question. "What color is this

sensation?" Accept the first response that comes to mind.

5. Now ask, "What size is this sensation?" Again, go with the first answer that comes to mind.

6. Now ask yourself, "Does this sensation have a texture to it? Is it smooth, rough, soft, or hard?"

7. Now, search the body for a sensation that is not relaxed, calm, or pleasant. Perhaps it has tension, pressure, heaviness, or hardness to it.

8. Now, just as with the pleasant sensation, inquire about the color, size, and texture of this sensation.

9. Using your awareness, allow yourself to imagine that the qualities of the unpleasant sensation taking on the qualities of the pleasant sensation. If the pleasant sensation had a green color, imagine the color of the unpleasant sensation turning green. If the texture of the pleasant sensation was soft, imagine the unpleasant sensation growing soft, and so on.

10. Take your time and transfer the qualities of the pleasant sensation to the unpleasant sensation.

11. Place your attention on the unpleasant sensation. Has it changed? Does it seem more pleasant as a result of transferring the positive qualities? If not, continue to practice this meditation.

Exercise 14

Our feelings inform us whether we are moving toward or away from our integrity as a human being. When we do not trust our feelings, we are unable to trust ourselves. This next meditation demonstrates how our feelings change with changes in our perceptions.

1. Sit down, close your eyes, and relax.

2. Allow yourself to become silent and observe the thoughts, feelings, emotions, and sensations that arise. Allow all of these phenomena to present themselves to your awareness.

3. Relax.

4. I want you to think of a situation that is currently causing you feelings of uneasiness, concern, or hurt. When you identify such a situation, allow yourself to focus on it. Relive the experience in your mind.

5. As you focus on the situation, become aware of the feelings that arise. Allow them to arise naturally.

6. Remember, your feelings are like a compass in that they have a message for you. They are telling you to move toward or away from that which you are focusing on.

7. When we are making decisions, taking actions, or focusing on things that bring about pleasant feelings, we know that we are on the right track and that we are consistent with our sense of integrity.

8. Conversely, when we have feelings that are unpleasant, it is a message that we are focusing on things that are inconsistent with our sense of integrity.

9. Ask yourself, "What can I do, believe, or focus on that will make me feel better about this situation?" Is there a decision that you need to make? Do you need let go of something? Do you need to question your thinking? Do you need to take time for yourself? Do you need to risk disappointing others?

10. Keep inquiring with yourself until you have identified a way to address the situation that leaves you with feelings of ease, relief, calm, or peace.

11. Whatever you come up with to address the situation, if it leads you to experience positive feelings, trust that it is the correct decision for you.

12. Your feelings are completely accurate and reliable at this moment in time. If your feelings regarding your solution or the situation change, honor them as well. Be sure not to confuse your feelings with your thoughts or beliefs. Your feelings are reliable, but your thoughts and beliefs are not.

13. If you are unable to find a way to make yourself feel better, that is okay, too. Allow yourself to remain with the feelings. Honor them by fully accepting them.

14. Accepting our feelings and being at peace with them is an act of self-love and an indication of integrity.

15. This is the end of the meditation. Please remain in your stillness for as long as you like.

Chapter 6: Meditation on the Self

In this book, you engaged in exercises for increasing your awareness of the nature of experience, thoughts, emotions, and feelings.

The purpose of these activities was to move you toward the realization that the phenomena of the mind and body are in constant flux and that who you are is the observer of these phenomena. Through this observation, we can arrive at the realization that the nature of who we are is beyond the phenomenal.

The more we lift the veils of illusions that are created by the mind, the closer we come to understanding our true nature. It is this understanding that will liberate you from the limiting thinking that impedes your ability to attract the wealth that you desire.

The following meditative exercises are the most profound of all, for they involve inquiring about the nature of who you are. By continually practicing these meditative exercises, you have an opportunity to make the most profound discovery a human can ever make. However, making this discovery requires that you be willing to let go of all of your beliefs about yourself.

Self-Inquiry
Exercise 15

Anytime we ask ourselves a question, we are engaging in inquiry. You will now engage in self-inquiry or the inquiry into the nature of your existence.

1. Sit down in a comfortable position and close your eyes.
2. Place your attention on your breath as you breathe. Feel it as it courses through your body.
3. Take on an attitude of complete allowing, that whatever arises in this meditation you will have complete acceptance of it.
4. Observe the perceptions, thoughts, sensations, feelings, and emotions that arise from you. Allow them to come and go on their own accord. All you need to do is to be aware of them.
5. You are the observer of thought, sensation, perception, emotions, and feeling. You are the one that is aware of experience. But who are you? You refer to yourself as "I." Who is this "I?"
6. Can you find where this "I" is located? Is it in your body? Is it in your heart?
7. The word "phenomenal" means something that can be seen, thought, touched, heard, or detected. Any response that you give to these questions is also phenomenal.

8. Anything that you experience and everything you know is phenomenal.

9. Even if you experience space, a sense of emptiness, or bliss, you are none of these. Space, emptiness, and bliss can be detected by you.

10. Your experiences come in and out of awareness. Who is observing experience coming in and out of awareness? Are you coming in and out of awareness?

11. Your emotions and feelings are constantly changing. Is your sense of being, the sense that you exist, constantly changing?

12. Any responses that you give to these questions is also observed, and there is a knowing of it. What is aware of this? What is observing this?

13. When answering this question, do not rely on your thinking. You will not get an answer.

14. Do not use your imagination or mind. Neither of these will answer this question.

15. Do not put any effort into answering this question. Just observe and be allowing. Continue asking yourself this question. Continue to inquire within.

16. The question of who you are is more important than the answer. Pursuing this question will lead to you experiencing the answer. You cannot know the answer; you can only experience it.

17. Whatever you are aware of cannot be you, for you are the awareness itself.

18. Who you are does not arise or fade. Who you are has no sense of identity or personality.

19. Who you are has no color, shape, or texture. Who you are never changes; it is eternally present.

20. Who you are cannot be experienced. Who you are is awareness itself. Just as a ray of light cannot shine on itself, the awareness that is you cannot observe itself. But you have a knowing that you exist.

21. Though you cannot perceive yourself, you can perceive that which you are not.

22. You are not your experience of life, nor are you your experience of yourself.

23. The more you discover that which you are not, the closer you will come to realizing who you are.

24. This is the end of this meditation. Allow yourself to remain in silence for as long as you desire.

Exercise 16

1. Sit in a comfortable position and close your eyes.

2. Allow yourself to follow your breath during inhalation and exhalation. Place your attention on your breath. Feel it as it courses through your body.

3. Take on an attitude of complete allowing, that whatever arises in this meditation that you have complete acceptance of it.
4. Observe the perceptions, thoughts, sensations, feelings, and emotions that arise from you. Allow them to come and go on their accord. All you need to do is be aware of them
5. Allow yourself to release all desires for effort, discovery, or any expectations of what you should be experiencing.
6. Allow your life to flow through you unhindered. Whatever arises within you, let it be. No action by you is required.
7. Allow yourself to sink into the depths of your being. Feel the sense of lightness and spaciousness within you.
8. You may experience a pleasant, warm sensation. Enjoy them and allow yourself to sink into these sensations.
9. Thought, emotions, and sensations will continue to arise. Allow them to be. Stay in the stillness of your being.
10. Anything that you experience is merely a projection of who you are. You are not your projections. You are the awareness of your projections.
11. Who you are cannot be observed or felt. Who you are has no shape, size, color, or sensation.
12. Who you are cannot be perceived or imagined. You can only know that which you are not.

13. You are like a movie screen, and your experiences are like the movie projected on it.

14. When we watch a movie, the movie and the screen seem to be one. There is no thought of the screen. We are only interested in the movie.

15. The movie is not the screen, and you are not your experience. Who you are is the invisible and undetectable screen that is behind all of experience.

16. Allow the movie of your experience to play before you. You are the awareness of them.

17. Who you are cannot be experienced, but you, the awareness, knows of experience.

18. All of experience in all of its diversity and form depends on your awareness for it to exist.

19. Experience arises from awareness and consciousness.

20. You are not your experience, but you can be found in all of experience.

21. At the level of consciousness, we are not separate from anything.

22. At the level of consciousness, our being merges into oneness.

23. At the level of the mind, we experience separateness.

24. All of this is happening without our involvement. This is ultimate reality, the union of non-duality and duality.

25. The mind or ego resists ultimate reality. It wants to dictate how life should be. But, the mind arises from

consciousness as well. It makes it possible for your sense of self to experience the world.

26. Simply allow life and experience to happen. There is nothing to control or change.

27. Everything that is happening was meant to happen.

28. Let go of all intentions, outcomes, strategies, and plans.

29. Let go of your memories, dreams, or thoughts on the future.

30. All mental and physical activity is experienced through consciousness

31. You are not your mental and physical activity.

32. You are the observer of mental and physical activity.

33. You are not the one who is meditating or doing self-inquiry. You are the observer of the one who is meditating and doing self-inquiry.

34. This is how consciousness experiences itself. It learns about itself through experiencing itself as a physical body and mind, a physical body and mind that has experienced.

35. You are informing consciousness through your experience and consciousness is providing you with the experience.

36. Do not resist any of this. Embrace it and surrender to it. This is true freedom, joy, and happiness.

37. This is the end of this meditation. Allow yourself to remain in silence for as long as you desire.

Chapter 7: The Law of Attraction and Money

The previous chapters focused on the nature of consciousness and experience, and a variety of exercises were provided for you to experience what would otherwise be theoretical. There is a reason why we spent most of this book on these topics.

The only reason why we experience difficulty in attracting money into our lives is that we are personalizing our experience of the mind and body. In other words, we are still under the illusion that somehow we are separate from what we want. It is these beliefs that are preventing us from experiencing the object of our intentions.

Of all the areas of our lives, few affect us as profoundly as money. Whether it is an abundance or a lack of it, money can have a powerful emotional impact on us.

Whether rich or poor, money plays a dominant role in the consciousness of most people. Because of this, we have developed strong beliefs and attitudes about money. Here are just a few examples of the more common ones:

- Money is the root of all evil.
- Money does not grow on trees.

- The desire for money is not spiritual.
- Most rich people got that way by taking advantage of others.
- It is selfish to ask for things that we cannot afford.
- I cannot become financially successful because I have too many things stacked against me.
- It takes money to make money.
- I do not deserve to be wealthy.

All of these beliefs were developed in response to a misunderstanding of money. They point to the mistaken belief that money has inherent power or value, or that money causes us to behave in a certain way.

Money is just a means to measure the exchange of value. If I pay a merchant $50 for a product, then both the vendor and I have agreed that the product is worth $50.

The value of money is purely subjective and established by the government. Its value is subject to change during periods of inflation. The mistake that many people make is that they focus on making money, which has no inherent value, instead of focusing on the value that they have to offer, which creates money.

Money is made when we find a way to create value for others and they are willing to compensate us for it.

There are people who have accumulated millions of dollars only to lose it all. Many of these individuals were able to rebuild their fortunes. On the other hand, there are people who live out their lives in financial scarcity despite their desire for money.

The only difference between these two groups of people are the beliefs that they hold. While it is true that some people have the resources and opportunities that others may lack, that alone is not the cause for the discrepancy between these two groups. There are plenty of people who started off with nothing but built fortunes.

Whether we are aware of it or not, our financial situation is the result of the Law of Attraction. The rich person who lost their money rebuilt their fortune because of their sense of certainty that they could do so. They had that sense of certainty because they experienced wealth before. It is that sense of certainty that allowed them to attract the opportunities to generate wealth into their lives.

For the person who lives out their life in scarcity, wealth is an abstract idea while scarcity is their daily experience. By focusing on their daily experience, they create an opposing force that works against their intentions for money. Thus, they continue to attract scarcity into their lives.

Interestingly, even the wealthy have a sense of scarcity, which is why some people accumulate millions and then lose it. As stated before, they were able to accumulate their fortune because of the beliefs that they held.

However, it is also their beliefs that cause them to lose their wealth. Like a thermostat, their limiting beliefs kicks in when they reach a certain income level, causing them to self-destruct financially.

They recover their losses because their empowering beliefs become activated. If they do not become aware of their limited beliefs, they will continue this cycle of wealth and loss.

When our dominant belief is that we can create wealth, regardless of our current situation, we can attract wealth into our lives provided that we apply ourselves and find a way to create value for others.

Conversely, if our dominant belief is that we will never move beyond financial struggle, that belief will attract the conditions that support it.

The difference between wealth and poverty has less to do with money and opportunity than it has to do with mindset. Henry Ford, Steve Jobs, Oprah Winfrey, J.K. Rowling, and Chris Gardner are just a few examples of people who came from very modest beginnings or even homelessness only to generate fortunes as adults.

Regardless of your story, your life conditions do not determine your ability to become financially successful. Rather, your life condition is a reflection of where you are placing your attention.

What is receiving the greater amount of your attention, your beliefs about your current situation or your sense of certainty that you can create wealth? The following sequence of exercises will guide you to guiding your focus toward attracting money. The steps include:

- Examine your beliefs about money
- Knowing yourself
- Identifying your qualifications
- Identifying needs
- Coming up with a winning idea and the Law of Attraction
- Attracting money using the Law of Attraction

Examine your Beliefs about Money

Exercise 17

Write out a list of all of your beliefs about money. If needed, refer to the examples in the earlier part of this chapter. When you write your list, do not make it an intellectual exercise. Instead, write whatever comes to mind.

When you have completed list, review each belief. If the belief does not make you feel empowered, draw a line through it and create a new belief that both resonates with and empowers you.

Note: Refer to the Exercise 6 in Chapter 6 for instructions on how to install your new belief.

Example:

Old belief: Money does not grow on trees.

New belief: Money grows from the ideas that I foster and pursue.

Knowing yourself

Exercise 18:

Money manifests when we create value for others by fulfilling an unmet need. When the value that you provide also aligns with your passion and joy, you have a winning formula.

Take time to reflect on what you enjoy doing. Think about what makes you happy or passionate. If there is something that you enjoy doing, then odds are you are also good at it. Make a list of all the things that you enjoy doing. It could be as simple as talking to being as complex as repairing computers.

Identify your qualifications

Exercise 19

Once you have made a list of the things that you enjoy doing, your next step is to make a list of all of your skills, talents, and knowledge base.

Skills are considered those abilities that you had to learn. For example:

- Accounting
- Repairing cars
- Scuba diving

Talents are those abilities that come naturally to you. They did not require any learning. Examples:

- Being compassionate
- Having a sense of humor
- Being persuasive
- Being athletic

Knowledge bases include the knowledge that you gained from formal education, training, or from being self-taught.

Identifying needs

Exercise 20:

This exercise involves identifying an unmet need. This need can be local, national, or global. Think of needs as problems, which can vary in magnitude.

Problems can be as minor as forgetting where you left your keys or glasses to being as relevant as water or energy shortages. Make a list of all the unmet needs that are meaningful to you.

Coming up with a winning idea and the Law of Attraction

Exercise 21:

Take time to reflect on the information that you gleaned from previous exercises. Can you come up with an idea that fuses all of those components together? Coming up with a winning idea can take time and research. If you find yourself unable to come up with an idea, you can use the Law of Attraction.

The Law of Attraction will attract the ideas, people, and circumstances for manifesting a money-making enterprise. It is critical that you do the first three exercises before turning to the Law of Attraction.

The information that you gain from these exercises will clarify your intentions. To attract a winning idea, do the following:

1. Review your work from the previous exercises in this chapter.
2. After reviewing the list, create an intention. For example:
    a. I will find an idea that addresses a need and creates happiness for all involved.
    b. I will find a way to align my joys and strengths with service to others.

    c. I will attract the people and circumstances that will allow me to successfully serve others.

3. Enter your meditation. When you reach a calm state, release your intention. Upon releasing your intention, give up all attachment to it. Simply continue to live your life.

4. Repeat this meditation until your request is manifested.

Attracting money using the Law of Attraction
Exercise 22

The following is a supplementary meditation that can be used to enhance the effects of the previous one. It was previously stated that we do not want money.

Rather, we want what money will give us. When you know what you want from money, do the following:

1. Sit down in a comfortable position, close your eyes, and breathe normally.
2. Place your attention on your breath by focusing on the sensations of it traveling in and out of your body.
3. As your focus on your breath, you will experience the appearance of thoughts. When they appear, simply ignore them and return your attention back to your breath.

4. If you keep your focus on your breath, there will come the point when you can maintain your awareness of it without any effort. When you reach this stage, think about how you would feel emotionally if you had the money that you desired. Experience these emotions as entirely as possible.

5. Imagine what you would see if you had the money that you desired.

6. Imagine what you would touch if you had the money that you desired.

7. Imagine what you would hear if you had the money that you desired.

8. Make these experiences as real as possible, making them more intense whenever possible, and then let them go.

9. When you are ready, awake from your meditation.

Chapter 8: Law of Attraction Mindset

As previously stated, everything in this universe has a vibrational quality. The dominant vibration in our life attracts manifestations of like kind into our life. If we give attention to our beliefs of limitation, difficulty, scarcity, or lack, then the vibrations of these beliefs inform consciousness that we want more of it.

It is no more difficult for consciousness to manifest $10,000 than it is to manifest a quarter. What hampers our ability to manifest is our resistance. We express resistance when we experience doubt about our ability to manifest.

To attract money, we need to raise our vibration so that our lives are conducive to receiving money.

The mistake that many people make is that they try to raise their vibration through techniques that are designed to be "one size fits all," or they do not sincerely believe what they are telling themselves as they try to raise their vibration.

I could meditate and repeat affirmations all day of how I want $10,000. However, if any part of me harbors doubt, I most likely will not manifest that $10,000. Now, if I meditated and repeated affirmation of how I want a quarter, I most likely would manifest a quarter. Why the difference? I am a lot more confident that I can manifest a quarter than I am manifesting $10,000.

However, there is another component that makes a difference, which is detachment. A quarter is not too meaningful to me, so I will not give much thought about it after I express my intentions for its manifestation. The same is not true of the $10,000.

I want that $10,000, and you better believe that I will be thinking about it long after I express my intentions for its manifestation. So, how can we overcome these obstacles and communicate our intentions for money effectively? The answer to this question is incredibly simple, as you will find in the next chapter.

Chapter 9: How to Remove Resistance

As previously stated, our feelings are our direct connection to consciousness, or our essential selves. When we are not experiencing happiness or peace, we are out of alignment with our essential self. When we experience these feelings, then we are in alignment. One of the challenges that many of us have is that we often avoid experiencing our feelings.

We have become experts in distracting ourselves to avoid experiencing them. We avoid experiencing our feelings because we fear or do not trust them. When we distance ourselves from our feelings, we distance ourselves from the rest of the universe.

The best thing that we can do to increase our ability to manifest is to start becoming more aware of our feelings and honoring them. When we learn to accept our feelings, both negative and positive, we are not only honoring them but honoring ourselves.

When we go against our feelings, we go against our Internal Guidance System. When we learn to trust our feelings, we regain our alignment with consciousness and rebuild trust in ourselves.

The Law of Attraction is a function of our focus. When we resist anything in life, we are giving it our focus. It is for this reason that we often attract that which we do not want. By removing our resistance, we can focus on what we want while maintaining our alignment with our essential self. The way we remove our resistance is through acceptance.

The principle of acceptance is often misunderstood, especially among the spiritual community. The practice of acceptance does not mean that we try to convince ourselves that things are okay or that they do not matter. To do so would dishonor our feelings. Rather, the spirit of acceptance is that we accept the existence of everything that we are experiencing in our lives. It means not to deny or resist those things that we find unpleasant.

When we can accept the existence of everything that enters our life, we create the space to give our focus to what we want. By doing so, the consciousness does not receive the mixed messages that resistance provides.

Letting Go and Allowing

I hope that by now that you realize that nothing about your experience is permanent. Your thoughts, feelings, and sensations are in constant flux. There is nothing in your experience that does not arise from within you. So what are you holding on to? What are you trying to control? This next meditation is about allowing.

Exercise 23

1. Sit down, make yourself comfortable, and relax. If you would like, you may close your eyes for now.
2. Allow yourself to relax as you focus on your breath. Place your attention on your breath as it enters your body, travels through your body, and then leaves it as you exhale.
3. Breathe normally, without exerting any effort. Relax.
4. Allow yourself to develop a sense of total acceptance. Be totaling allowing of whatever appears in your awareness.
5. Do not judge, evaluate, or analyze anything that you experience.
6. Do not hold any expectations for what you should be experiencing.
7. Do not search for, imagine, or create anything. Simply observe.
8. If unpleasant or uncomfortable thoughts, feelings, or sensation arise, let them be.
   Allow them to come to your awareness. Do not try to change them or replace them with something that is more pleasant or positive.

9. If you feel numbness or a sense of dullness, allow this.

10. You cannot do anything wrong. Whatever you are experiencing, this is the right experience for you.

11. Allow experience to flow through your awareness without any interference.

12. There is nothing for you to do, change, or believe in. Simply be aware of all that presents itself.

13. This is the end of this meditation. Allow yourself to remain in silence for as long as you desire.

A Day without Resistance

We all have done things that went against how we felt, and we have been doing so since we were small children. We learned early on the consequences of not meeting the expectations of our parents. As we grew older, we increasingly faced situations that demanded our allegiance. Out of social pressure, we often gave in to those demands at the expense of how we felt. The people in our lives, jobs, and societal expectations have all conspired to perpetuate the dishonoring of our feelings. The following exercises are intended to guide you back to honoring your feelings.

Exercise 24

In this exercise, you will commit to engaging only in those activities that are consistent with how you feel. If you do not feel like doing something, then do not do it. If you feel like doing something, do it! If you find yourself having trouble doing this exercise for a whole day, then do it for a shorter time, even if it is for just 20 minutes, and then extend that time until you can do it for a whole day.

Obviously, there are things that we all need to do which we would rather not. Not doing them would be irresponsible. In cases such as these, use the following guidelines:

- Change your perspective of the task that is creating resistance in you by focusing on all the benefits that you would gain by completing it.
- Find ways to change the way that you approach doing the task by making it more enjoyable for you. For example: Listen to your favorite music while doing yard work or invite a friend over to do your taxes together.
- If none of the previous techniques work to lower your resistance, do not take on the task until you have come to accept the fact that it needs to be done and that you are willing to do it.

It is important to note that the previous exercise has nothing to do with the task itself. Instead, it is about our resistance to the task. Nothing in life has inherent meaning to it. It is us who projects meaning onto life.

Chapter 10: The Pathway to Reconnection

Earlier, I offered the example of manifesting $10,000 versus a quarter. I indicated that it is easier to attract a quarter than it is to attract $10,000 because of our resistance and attachment toward manifesting the $10,000. In the previous chapter, we discussed ways to reduce your resistance. In this chapter, you will learn a technique to increase your vibration by moving up the vibrational scale. What is amazing is how simple this step is.

To enter the space where intentional manifesting occurs, we need to not only reduce our resistance but raise our vibration. The process for doing this involves focusing on the things in your life that bring you enjoyment or a sense of well-being and becoming fully associated with the feeling and emotions that accompany it. I will outline the steps to this process by using myself an example. If I wanted to attract $10,000, I would reflect on what is it that I enjoy or what makes me feel good. My thoughts may be:

- "I enjoyed the time that I took just to relax and not do anything."

- "I enjoyed getting up early this morning and seeing the sunrise and experiencing the quiet calm of desert."
- "I love seeing my wife's smile and hearing her laugh."
- "I am enjoying the sense of peace that I experience when I practice accepting everything that enters my life."
- "I feel revitalized when I think about how I can use the manifesting process to improve my family's life."
- "I love the sense of peace that comes from knowing that I am supported and loved by the universe."

By identifying those aspects of my life that sincerely bring me happiness or comfort, I am raising my vibration. By making this a continuous practice in my life, I am not only raising my vibration, but I am maintaining it.

When I maintain a high vibration, then all that is left for me to do is to express my intention for the $10,000. After I express my intention, I return my focus back to those things that bring me happiness. My intentions will be registered with my essential self because I am in alignment with my essential self.

It is important to take note that my focus was not on the $10,000. Rather, it was on those things that I already enjoy. My intention for the $10,000 was like a seed that was planted in the fertile ground of my sense of appreciation and happiness.

Powering up your intentions

This following exercise will take the power of your intentions to the next level:

Exercise 25

Sit down in a comfortable position, close your eyes, and breathe normally.

1. Place your attention on your breath by focusing on the sensations of it traveling in and out of your body.
2. As your focus on your breath, you will experience the appearance of thoughts. When they appear, simply ignore them and return your attention back to your breath.
3. If you keep your focus on your breath, there will come the point when you can maintain your awareness of it without any effort. When you reach this stage, do the following:
    a. Imagine how you would feel if you had the amount of money that you desired. Experience these emotions as fully as possible.
    b. Imagine what you would see if you had the money that you desired. How would you spend it?

c. Imagine what you would touch if you had the money that you desired. What would it feel like?

d. Imagine what you would hear if you had the money that you desired. If you could buy what you wanted, what would it sound like?

e. Make these experiences as real as possible and intensify the feelings.

4. When you are ready, awake from your meditation.

What you accomplished through this meditation was utilizing all of your senses to experience what you would get from the money you desired as though it was already yours. By making your desired experience real for you today, you are informing consciousness of what you want to be manifested in your life. By focusing on the feelings of what you desire, you are becoming a vibrational match for it to come into your life.

Perform this meditation daily until you can effortlessly experience that which you desire. This can be accomplished by taking time during your day to rehearse this meditation in your mind by focusing on what you desire and fully experiencing the feelings.

By doing this continuously, you will eventually condition yourself to experience these feelings anytime you think of what you desire from the money.

Chapter 11: What Do You Really Want?

Though this book has been focusing on how to use the Law of Attraction to attract money, it is time to move toward higher levels of awareness and discover the truth of what you want! I am confident in saying that I know something about you that you may not. What I know about you is that you do not want money. You want what you believe money will give you. Money is just paper. What you want is the emotions and feelings that you believe you experience by having money. Here is an exercise for discovering what you truly want:

Exercise 26

1. Ask yourself the question "If I had the amount of money that I desire, what would it mean to me?
Examples of responses could be:
   - A sense of security
   - A better life
   - Not having to work
   - Being able to buy whatever I want
2. For example, my reply may be that having the amount of money that I desire would mean that I would have enough money to save for the future.
3. For the next step, I would repeat the first question but incorporate my response into the question:
4. What would having enough money to save mean to me?

5. Having enough money to save would make me feel more secure. I would know that the money is there if I need it.
6. What would having a sense of security mean to me?
7. Having a sense of security would give me peace of mind.

Based on this example, my desire for money is not my root desire. My real desire is the peace of mind that I believe money would give me. However, even this root desire is just an illusion.
There are people with fortunes who lack peace of mind.

In fact, there are people with more money than they will ever need who are full of anxiety and fear. Conversely, there are people in third world countries who live with a sense of peace and acceptance.

Ultimately, at the essential level, anything that you could desire already exists in your life. To realize this requires looking inward and exploring your inner world. It is through exploring your inner world that you move in the direction of self- discovery and the discovery of your essential self. From higher a perspective, the Law of Attraction is a tool that the universe uses to demonstrate to you that who you are is more than your sense of being a person.

Chapter 12: Intentions and Life Purpose

We have covered a lot of information on manifesting. We discussed the obstacles that many people encounter when attempting to manifest, including overly identifying with the mind and body functions, our limiting beliefs, not being aware of our feelings, and resistance. But even if someone was to steer clear of these obstacles, they still may not get what they want if they lack clarity in their intentions and purpose.

In the previous chapter, we discussed the question, "What you truly want?" This chapter builds on that. We could do everything right, but if our intentions are not clear, we will not manifest what we want. I previously stated that no one wants money. Rather, we want what we believe money will give us. Your answer to the question "What money would give me?" will clarify your intentions and provide a valuable clue to second part of this chapter, which is your life purpose.

Intentions

Your intentions broadcast to consciousness that which you desire and want to experience in your life. There are certain guidelines to follow when creating your intentions:

- Get clarity on your intentions before you allow them to become part of your focus. As stated before, our intentions should not be for money. Rather, our intentions should be for what we believe money would give us. Refer to Exercise 5 in Chapter 6 to determine this.

- Make your intentions impersonal. To be effective, do not personalize your intentions. When we personalize our intentions, they may be driven by our egos and be fear-based. When our intentions are for the benefit of others, we liberate ourselves from the ego. Further, we come from a place that is not fear based. For example, instead of having the intentions, "I will get the job that I desire," make your intention, "I will get the job where I can create the greatest value for all those involved." This kind of intention focuses on our strengths and what we can give as opposed to what we want, which comes from a place of need.

- Avoid making your intentions too specific. Your intentions should be focused on the final result of what you want to experience in your life, not when or how it will happen. The intention, "I want to attract the conditions that will allow me to support my family," will be more effective than, "I want $30,000 by the end of the year." Again, it is not money that you want; it is what money would give you. The intent to attract those conditions that will support my family does not limit consciousness in how it can express itself to meet that need. Asking for $30,000 by the end of the year narrows the possibilities for consciousness to express itself.

Purpose in Life

Few people are born knowing their life's purpose. For most of us, our life's purpose involves a journey through life. However, this journey is not a journey of distance and time. Finding one's purpose in life involves a journey of going within.

Though the situations and circumstances of our lives may be what grab our attention, the true magic of discovering who we are is revealed from the depth of our lives. As author Parker J. Palmer stated: "'Before I can tell my life what I want to do with it, I need to listen to my life to tell me who I am." Ultimately, your life purpose is about what you are here to give.

Many people struggle in life because they do not have a sense of purpose. Conversely, there are just as many people who are actively seeking their purpose in life but are unable to find it. From higher perspectives of awareness, having a purpose in life is moot point. Our essential self, or consciousness, does not need a purpose in life.

At the level of your essential self, you are beyond any conceptual thought. It is only in our manifested form that the need for a purpose in life may appear. If you can live happily without knowing your purpose in life, do not worry about finding it. On the other hand, if you find a need to know your life's purpose, it is best that you do not get too serious about it and approach its discovery in a light-hearted way. I say this to you because your need to find your life's purpose does not come from your essential self. It comes from your mind. To say your life's purpose comes from the mind does not negate your sense of need for it. Instead, I'm making this statement to point out that you can be happy without it. The mind creates a need for finding our life's purpose out of its own dissatisfaction.

The mind is only happy when it can keep us on our toes. The mind is always looking for a job to do. Fear, excitement, guilt, worry, pride, arrogance, superiority, and inferiority are all job titles that the mind accepts. When we identify with our minds, we become the mind's co-worker and share in its responsibilities.

When you understand how our minds work, meaning that you are no longer obedient to it, your sense of purpose, if needed, will become self-evident. It will become self-evident because you will awaken to your unbounded potentiality. The unbounded potentiality that I speak of is your essential self and is expressed in your manifested being as your passions, talents, and strengths, which we will discover in the next section.

Finding your Life's Purpose

The steps for identifying your purpose in life are very similar to the steps for attracting money. Saying that finding your purpose in life and attracting money should share similar steps is not surprising because the manifestation process is the same for everything that we want to experience. The following are steps to find your purpose:

- Focusing inward
- Getting out there
- Focusing outward
- Realization
- Problem-solving

Focusing inward

Focusing inward is the first step in finding your life purpose because everything that we experience begins there. I know the world around me through my five senses. However, the information that I get from my five senses is synthesized and assembled from within me. It is from this conceptual place that I understand the world. Further, we already discussed that our feelings are our GPS to our alignment with our essential self.

Your life purpose does not have to be sought out because it has always existed within you. Rather than searching for your life's purpose, you want to take the time to experience it. We experience our life's purpose when we pay attention to our feelings.

The reason why we spent so much time on meditative exercises is that it is one of the best ways to gain awareness of our thoughts and feelings. By becoming aware of our thoughts and losing our identification with them, we can shift our focus to our feelings and listen to the message that they are sending us. Here is your first exercise to finding your life's purpose: Get a sheet of paper and a writing instrument.

Get into a meditative state. You can use any of the previous exercises, or you can use your own technique (Note: You may be able to do this exercise without going into meditation. If you find it difficult to recall past events, going into meditation can help).

When you are in a relaxed state, think of the times when you were the happiest. When you think of a specific time, try to remember:

- What were you were doing at the time?

- *Who was around you at the time?*
- What was it about this time that made it so enjoyable for you?
- *When you receive this information, write it down.*
- When you are finished recording, go back into meditation and think of another time when you were at your happiest.
- *Repeat this process until you can no longer recall memories of your happy times.*

When you have completed your list, I want you to think about your passions, strengths, skills, and knowledge base.

Passions

Think about what creates a sense of passion in you. Make a list of all the things that give you a sense of passion.

Strengths

For your strengths, think about the strong points of your character. What is it that you are known for? Think of your strong points as those aspects of you that come naturally to you. They are effortless. Examples could be:

- Your sense of humor
- Your patience
- Your sensitivity
- Your ability to persuade others

- Your athletic ability
- Your compassion

Skills

Unlike your strengths, your skills are those things that you do well as a result of previous training or education that you had. Make a list of your skills. Examples of skills may be:

- Computer skills
- Debate skills
- Sales skills
- Supervisory skills
- Writing skills
- Administrative skills

Note: There may be some overlap between your strengths and skills. If you encounter this overlap, place that item in the category that you believe it fits best.

Knowledge Base

Your knowledge base is the information that you have gained through past formal education or training. Your knowledge base differs from the previous category in that your knowledge may not always be evident since it may not express itself in your actions. For this exercise, think of your knowledge base as being the intellectual part of you. Make a list of your knowledge areas.

Examples are:

- Being philosophical
- Legal expertise
- Knowledge of design principles
- Theoretical knowledge

When you have completed your lists, review them. You will use them later. For now, you are ready to go on to the next step.

Getting Out There

Remember that you are the physical manifestation of your essential self, which is consciousness. You appeared in your manifested form for the purpose of experiencing. Like anything else in life, we discover our life's purpose through experiencing contrast in this world. This step of the process is called *Getting Out There* because that is the only way you can discover your life's purpose.

Your instruction for this step of the process is to expose yourself to as many different experiences as you can. It means challenging yourself by stepping out of your comfort zone. Try something that you have never done before out of fear. Try something that you have never done before out of the belief that it was of no interest to you. Try something that you have never done before out of your concern over what others might think. You came to this Earth to experience and expand consciousness. It is only by doing so that you will be able to tap into the discovery of what you are here to give.

For the first half of my life, I was of a strictly scientific mindset. I had no interest whatsoever in spiritual matters. For me, if I could not examine it, measure it, or observe it, I could not give credibility to it. If someone had spoken to me about the Law of Attraction, I would have been polite about it. I would pretend to listen while my thoughts would be elsewhere.

Today, I am writing about it based on personal experience. How did I make the jump from being a devotee of science to an explorer of consciousness? I started to expose myself to experiences that I avoided before. I started to read books about the subject, I listened to experts in the field of consciousness, and I started meditating.

When you start exposing yourself to new experiences, you want to enter them the same way that you were instructed in the various exercises in this book. You want to be open-minded, be accepting of whatever you experience, and not have any expectations. Just as in meditation, allow yourself to be immersed in the experience.

Focusing Outward

In the first step of this process, you went inward and did a personal assessment of yourself. In the previous step, you exposed yourself to different experiences. In this step, *Focusing Outward,* you are going to do another assessment. Unlike your personal assessment, your assessment in this step of the exercise is going to be focused on the world around you. You are going to assess the unmet needs of those around you. The need could be a need within your family, or in your neighborhood, community, state, country, or in another part of the world.

Those who create wealth do so by providing an answer to a problem, or they find a better answer to a problem. Examples of problems could be as simple as finding a way to prevent people from losing their eyeglasses to finding a way to address water shortages on a mass scale. For this exercise, stay alert to the opportunities for making a difference in the lives of others.

Realization

In the previous steps, you assessed your passions, strengths, and other abilities. You then exposed yourself to new experiences. In the previous step, you assessed the unmet needs of others. Now it is time for realization. This is the step when you try to connect the dots. You do this by selecting an unmet need, and you think of ways you can utilize your passion and strengths to make a difference for those who are experiencing that need.

I know of a veterinarian who recognized a need in her community. Many people who have pets are unable to afford traditional veterinary care. This situation poses numerous problems. There are pet owners who love their pets and have to see them suffer. Because their pets are not getting spayed or neutered, there is a problem with unwanted births. Obviously, this veterinarian had the knowledge base and skills to meet this need. More importantly, she has the passion for helping others.

This veterinarian started a mobile service where she travels around the county to provide pet owners with veterinary care at a fraction of the cost of traditional care. The result is that she has loyal customers throughout the county, her overhead is minimal compared to other veterinarians, and she is doing what she loves.

Your exercise for this section is to determine how you can apply your passions and strengths to the unmet need that you selected.

Problem Solving

Problem-solving is the step where you take the results of the previous exercise and start developing a plan on how you would put it into action. You want to ask yourself questions like:

- Is there someone already doing what I have thought of? If so, what could I learn from them? More importantly, how can I improve on what they are already doing?
- Who do I need to talk to?
- What resources will I need?
- Where can I get help to write a business plan?
- What are the risks involved in this venture?
- How can I mitigate these risks?
- What legal or regulatory requirements do I need to be aware of?
- How can I recruit the support of others to make my vision real?

It is important to note that this five-step process is a guideline and does not need to be followed in this order. You will most likely find yourself experiencing situations that do not follow a neat order as I have outlined, which is perfectly okay, but you want to incorporate all of the steps at some point in the process. Additionally, many of these steps may present themselves to you simultaneously.

The main thing to understand is that once you start this process, your intentions will attract the people, resources, and situations that will help you move forward. In fact, this process is providing a structure for you to focus on. It is your focus that informs your essential self to what you will need in any given situation. When you give to others that which you want, you will experience what you are looking for in your life.

It deserves repeating the importance of drilling down into your desires and discovering what lies beneath. I may want more money because I believe that it will give me a sense of security. As long as I base my sense of security on the amount of money that I earn, then my sense of security is dependent upon something outside of myself.

Since everything that is outside of myself is subject to change, my sense of security will change as well. Let us say that you find a new job which triples your income. At first, you will be excited and happy with your new situation. You may increase your spending, raise your standard of living, and start building your savings. However, that increase in money can lead to a new sense of insecurity. You may become insecure about your ability to maintain your new lifestyle. You may feel insecure about losing your money and want to protect it. All of the potential concerns that arise from your increased income exist due to the illusion that money will give you what you are looking for.

Now let us look at a different scenario. Let us say you took the time to explore your beliefs. You identified your limiting beliefs and changed them into empowering ones. You also increased your awareness to the nature of your thoughts, emotions, and feelings. You realize that your essential nature is greater than these mental functions. You also reduced your resistance toward life. Doing all of these things would lead to increasing your sense of security regardless of how much money you had. Further, this sense of security would exist independently of what was happening around you.

Because your experience of life has changed, you feel the desire to help others feel more secure in their lives. This desire to share becomes your life purpose. Because you are in alignment with your essential self, your sense of security grows exponentially. It is fueled by your focus on others. Focusing on your intentions will lead to the unfolding of your life's purpose.

Chapter 13: Your Ultimate Desire

At the surface level, this book appears to be about money and the Law of Attraction. However, the true intent of this book is far more profound. The intent of this book is to act as a pointer to a source of wealth that is beyond anything that you can grasp intellectually. As repeatedly stated in this book, you do not want money. You want what money can give you.

However, even this statement can be easily misunderstood. You may say that you want money because it will give you a greater sense of security, that it will allow you to take care of your family, or that it will allow you to make a difference in this world.

Previously, you were asked to drill into your thinking to find the root cause for your desire for money. However, even this exercise will fall short of reaching your ultimate desire. Regardless of our reasons for wanting more money, the root cause for wanting money is the emotional state that we experience. In fact, our emotional state is a cause for us desiring anything. However, even our emotional state is not the ultimate cause for our desire.

Our emotional desire is not for the attaining of anything. At the deepest level, our emotional desire is to return home.

Throughout this book, it was stated that we are multidimensional beings in that we are the manifestation of consciousness. We are simultaneously a physical and non-physical being. The essence of who we are is non-physical; our experience of ourselves is our physical aspect. We took on our manifested form so that we could experience the world and expand consciousness, which we do through experience.

For us to experience, we need to experience a sense of separateness. Ultimately, anything that you could ever want is rooted in your desire to leave your sense of separateness behind and return home. You want to return to your essential self where there is a sense of oneness, wholeness, and eternal peace.

Every challenge that we have as human being, be it at the individual or collective level, is due to our confusing the world of objects to be the answer to our ultimate desire. Chasing objects, however, never works. If we are honest with ourselves, lasting happiness or fulfillment does not exist in the realm of form.

You may want to use the Law of Attraction to become a millionaire. Even if you become a millionaire, you will not achieve lasting happiness or fulfillment. Having a million dollars only creates new challenges, insecurities, and desires.

The reason for this is that your ultimate desire can only be quenched when you return home.

The only way to return home is to develop the qualities that your essential self inherently possesses. What are the qualities of your essential self? If you practice the exercises and guidance in this book, you will eventually experience them for yourself. In fact, there is no way you cannot experience them if you are sincere in your desire to pursue your truth. However, here are some clues regarding the qualities that I speak of:

- Appreciation
- Kindness to all, especially yourself
- Compassion to all, especially for yourself
- Non-judgment
- Acceptance of yourself and others
- And most of all, love

It may sound trite, but love is your essential self. When I speak of love, I am not referring to romantic love or even the love that we have for family. The kind of love that I speak of is unconditional. Unconditional love is the acceptance and embracement for all of life.

To reach the state of awareness that I have just described may seem to be a daunting task or an unrealistic goal. Should this thought occur to you, I have good news for you. Ignore that thought! Everything that has been discussed in this book about higher perspectives of awareness, and your essential self, already exists within you. In fact, there is no way for you to not possess them.

The only reason why we do not experience our deepest essence is that we have been conditioned from the time that we were born to focus on the world around us, not our inner world. We have spent our lives chasing shiny objects in that hopes that we will experience our ultimate desire.

It is because we have forgotten about our essential nature that this book offered so many meditative exercises. It is only when we take time to become still and silent that we can start to remember our deeper truths.

My guess is that you purchased this book because you believe having more money in your life will satisfy that which you are searching for. The good news is that you can find what you have been searching for, and have money, if you redirect your attention toward your inner realm. It is only in your inner realm that you will find the answers you have been looking for. In the next chapter, we will discuss what to do next!

Chapter 14: Making Sense of it All

You have been presented with a wealth of information and exercises in this book. This chapter is about your next step. To read this book and not look at it again would defeat its purpose. This book is intended to be a guide for you for as long as you seek out your ultimate fortune, which is the sense of peace that comes from aligning your life with your essential self. The following are some suggestions for getting the most out of your manifesting experience:

- Do not judge anything that you experience.
- Do not hold expectations of what should happen or of what should not happen.
- Allow everything that you experience to happen, and do not resist anything. Every thought, sensation, perception, or outwardly experience has its place. Everything that exists is intended to exist.
- No thought, feeling, or sensation can harm you. It is you that they owe their existence to.

Having said this, here are some suggestions regarding the content of this book:

- Make sure that you read the entire book and do each exercise at least once.

- When you have completed the book, take note of the exercises that resonated with you or felt right to you. You do not have to do every exercise in this book to achieve your desires. However, you will not know if these exercises are right for you unless you do them.

- Once you have selected the exercises that resonate with you, practice at least one of them each day. When I say to practice them each day, I do not mean to practice them in the traditional sense. Normally, practice is viewed as repeatedly doing something to improve. When it comes to meditation, there is nothing to improve! Meditation is about being still and quiet. Its purpose is to increase our awareness of the nature of the mind. Meditation should not require any effort other than getting yourself to do it. Each time you do a meditative exercise, treat is as though it is your first time doing it.

Once you become comfortable meditating, the following guidelines can be used to attract your desires:

- Develop a clear intention of what you want to attract.
- Make sure your intentions are aligned so that everyone who will be affected by them will benefit.

- Increase your vibration using meditations in this book, especially from Chapter 10, until you have reached a state of well-being.
- When you have reached a state of well-being, express your intention to the universe. When expressing your intention, express it through your emotional state as opposed to thinking about it intellectually. In other words, if you want to manifest $1,000, experience how you would feel if you already had $1,000. If you experience any sense of doubt during this process, refer to the exercises in Chapters 6 & 10.
- Take action that will move you toward the manifestation of your desire. If you desire is to manifest $1,000, what action can you take that will create the opportunities to receive it? Remember, you do not want $1,000. You want what it will give you. A great way to take action is to do the exercises in Chapter 11.
- It is crucial to understand that everything that you read in this book is just a pointer, a pointer that is pointing to your essential self and inviting you to follow.
- Do not get caught up with anything that you read in this book. Do not take anything written in this book as truth. There is no ultimate truth in the universe. What we believe to be truth is a product of the mind. Instead of seeking truth, seek that which resonates with you, that which brings you happiness.

- Use the information in this book to launch yourself into your inner journey. Let this book be a guide, not the pilot. It is up to you to determine what feels right for you and to honor it.

- Have the courage to trust your essential self, that part of you which is beyond your thoughts and sensations, and that part of you which you can only know intuitively.

Conclusion

We started this book with two metaphors, the man in the desert and King Midas, and so that is how we will end. In Greek mythology, there is Plato's Allegory of the Cave. There is a group of people who are imprisoned in a cave where they are chained. Against the wall of the cave, they see moving shadows.

The people of the cave believe that these shadows are living beings that also inhabit the cave. What they are not aware of is that there is a large fire at the entrance of the cave. Any time somebody walked by, between the fire and entrance of the cave, their shadow was projected onto the cave wall.

One of the people inside the cave is able to free himself from his chains and wanders outside of the cave. It is then that he realizes the truth of what he had been witnessing in the past. The shadows of the cave were illusionary. They were just representations of something greater.

Another metaphor is that of the clouds and sky. Of the two, the sky is greater due to its vastness. Additionally, the sky is non-changing, unlike the clouds, which are constantly taking on different shapes. Whatever the clouds do, the sky remains untouched.

I leave you with this final thought about your true nature and that of the phenomenal world, which includes money. As long as our sense of self is shaped or defined by the amount of money that we have, we are no better than the prisoner in the cave who believes the shadows are the real thing.

This is not only true about money, but also for anything else that is phenomenal. To define ourselves by anything that we experience, be it a thought, sensation, relationship, our jobs, or our possessions, is to identify with a shadow.

True success is achieved when we become like the sky. Like the sky, you are free. As the sky is unaffected by the clouds that travel through it. We should strive to discover that aspect of ourselves that is also unaffected by the clouds of thought, sensation, perception, and objects that float through our awareness.

What is required for this kind of liberation is to lose the personalizing of our experiences, including that of the Law of Attraction and money. Instead of viewing the Law of Attraction as a way to manifest our desires, I invite you to view it as a natural process of the universe, of which you bear witness to. To believe that we attract things into our lives is to reinforce our sense of separation.

The only way that you can attract something is if that which you want to attract is separate from yourself. Who you are at the non-phenomenal level is not separate from the universe. Rather, your essential self is the universe! You will experience greater expansion if you stay as an observer to all that enters and leaves your life. Every thought, sensation, and perception is just a visitor that passes through your awareness. You are the witness to their movement. They exist only because you exist!

What we refer to as the Law of Attraction is that of the world of existence continuously parading through our awareness. The world of existence is like a current moving through the expanse of the ocean, and you are the ocean. Learn to enjoy and appreciate every experience that enters your life. The clouds of pleasure, happiness, peace, sadness, fear, and grief, are the clouds that transverse your skies. Learn to view money, not as a measure of your success but a tool, a unit of exchange, in your encounters with other manifested beings. When you can live your life in this spirit, you will be wealthy regardless of your net worth!

Before You Go...

Upon achieving higher levels of awareness, it will become crystal clear to you that who we are is beyond our thoughts. As pure consciousness, we can manifest anything we want spontaneously without bigger effort.

In order to get there, get committed to getting to know your true self and removing resistance. Schedule your LOA rituals time and enjoy the exercises from this book.

We are all energy. Let's rise higher and enjoy the process!

I am very curious to hear back to you.

If you have a few moments, please share your thoughts in the review section of this book and let us know which exercise you found most helpful. Your honest review on Amazon would be much appreciated. It's you I am writing for and I would love to know your feedback.

Thanks You again for picking up this book and reading it to the very end. I am very grateful for You.

Happy Manifesting,

Elena G.Rivers

PS. Check out the next page for the special free offer I have created for you.

A Special Offer from Elena

Finally, I would like to invite you to join my private mailing list (my *VIP LOA Newsletter*). Whenever I release a new book, you will be able to get it at a discounted price (or sometimes even for free, but don't tell anyone 😊).

In the meantime, I will keep you entertained with a free copy of my exclusive LOA workbook that will be emailed to you when you sign up.

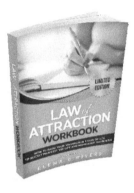

To join visit the link below now:

www.loaforsuccess.com/newsletter

After you have signed up, you will get a free instant access to this exclusive workbook (+ many other helpful resources that I will be sending you on a regular basis). I hope you will enjoy your free workbook.

If you have any questions, please email us at:
support@loaforsuccess.com

More Books written by Elena G.Rivers

Available at: www.loaforsuccess.com

Ebook – Paperback – Audiobook Editions Available Now

Law of Attraction for Amazing Relationships

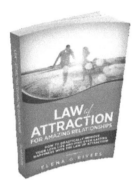

Law of Attraction for Weight Loss

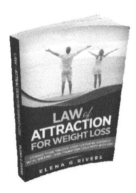

Law of Attraction-Manifestation Exercises

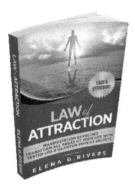

Law of Attraction to Make More Money

You will find more at:

www.loaforsuccess.com/books